IMAGES
of America
THE
CHEMUNG
VALLEY

IMAGES
of America
THE
CHEMUNG
VALLEY

Diane L. Janowski
and Allen C. Smith

ARCADIA
PUBLISHING

Copyright © 1998 by Diane L. Janowski and Allen C. Smith
ISBN 978-1-5316-0011-2

Published by Arcadia Publishing
Charleston, South Carolina

Library of Congress Catalog Card Number: 98-88253

For all general information contact Arcadia Publishing at:
Telephone 843-853-2070
Fax 843-853-0044
E-mail sales@arcadiapublishing.com
For customer service and orders:
Toll-Free 1-888-313-2665

Visit us on the Internet at www.arcadiapublishing.com

Cover Image: Citizens of Elmira stand in the flood waters on Water Street, March 1, 1902.

CONTENTS

Introduction		7
1.	Early Photographs	9
2.	Turn of the Century	45
3.	Years of Prosperity	107

Elmira's most prominent photographer, Elisha Van Aken, is seen here at work above the Chemung Valley. The photograph was taken by his son, Charles Van Aken, c. 1903.

INTRODUCTION

Elmira, New York, owes its existence and evolution to waterways. Christian Loop and John Hendy, the first settlers, dragged their flat bottom boats up the Chemung River to farm its fertile valley. Matthias Hollenback established the area's first trading post and mill near the junction of the river and Newtown Creek. The village grew toward the west. The opening of the Chemung Canal in 1832 hastened the development of the city. The Chemung River significantly flooded its banks four times, in 1889, 1902, 1946, and 1972. Each of these disasters dramatically affected the development of our neighborhoods, industry, government, agriculture, and transportation.

This is visual history of the citizens of this region using photographs from the permanent collection of the Chemung Valley History Museum. The period covered is c. 1860 to 1976. By no means is it the complete story. For a more thorough understanding of our history, readers may refer to *Our County and Its People, a History of the Valley and County of Chemung, from the Closing Years of the Eighteenth Century* by Ausburn Towner; *Chemung County, 1890–1975* by Thomas Byrne; and *Mark Twain's Elmira, 1870–1910* by Michelle L. Cotton. These volumes, the Chemung County Historical Society's Journals, and other publications are available at the Chemung Valley History Museum and the Steele Memorial Library in Elmira.

Criteria for inclusion of the photographs were aesthetic content, historic significance, and human interest. Elmira's earliest photographs were made near the canal, c. 1854. By the 1870s professional photographers were making excellent portraits of the inhabitants and their environs. With fine detail they recorded merchants in front of their stores, factory workers at their work stations, blacksmiths in front of liveries, families and pets on sidewalks in residential neighborhoods, and children on school steps. Families took their "Kodaks" on outings and picnics to Eldridge Park, Rorick's Glen, and Sullivan's Monument.

More often than not, the photographers have not signed the individual photographs, making attribution difficult. The following is a list of photographers whose works appear in this publication. We wish to acknowledge their contributions to the recorded history of the Chemung Valley.

Wells Crandall
Arthamese Denny
Eva Derby
Dan Driscoll
John Larkin
George Lian
Fred T. Loomis
Charles Lovell
Abram McFarlin
George Millspaugh
George Personius
Frank Ridall
Henry Sartor
Elisha and Charles Van Aken
Jacob C. Vetter
The staff photographers
of the *Elmira Advertiser*, *Sunday Telegram*, and *Star Gazette*

Whenever possible, we have researched the available information to name the subjects in the photographs and to learn their residences, workplaces, familial relationships, and entertainment pleasures. All of the photographs are site-specific and each has a noted location. We encourage readers to take their books with them in their travels around Elmira. Keep your book in your car.

We implore residents of our community to search their family's archives for representative photographs of the region and to give the originals or professional copies to the permanent collection of the Chemung Valley History Museum. As the turn of the century approaches we suggest that we all record the Chemung Valley as it is today for the enjoyment of future generations.

—Diane L. Janowski and Allen C. Smith

One
EARLY PHOTOGRAPHS

The Junction Canal connected the Chemung Canal in Elmira to the north branch of the Susquehanna Canal (a distance of 18 miles), just south of the Pennsylvania border. This c. 1854 photo was taken near the Rolling Mills in the area of the Washington Avenue Park.

"There is no use in denying the fact that the early settlers of the county were rude, rough, rollicking, often swearing, violent men . . . The early settlers loved to drink whisky, and they had lots of it." In this 1858 photo looking north on Lake Street, the famous "Paddy's Pig" roams freely. Elmira was "a mixture of Wildwest and Roots Flavor." (CCHS Journal.)

Young Elmirans sit on the spillway at State Street and the Chemung River watching the world go by around 1868. In winter, the canal had to close, but it provided a wonderful skating rink. In summer, the canal was a haven for fishermen waiting for a bite. Spring brought the breaking up of ice, broken locks, and rotted lumber. It might be June before the canal could maintain heavy traffic. Canal families lived on barges and traveled all summer. Canal boat captain was an important position.

The Chemung Canal took four years to build. Thomas Cook, the general contractor, designed the canal to be 4 feet deep, 42 feet wide, and 23 miles long. It opened for traffic in October 1833 with a big celebration as the first barge left the basin at State and Market Streets (shown behind the women in this photo from 1868). There were 49 locks between Elmira and Watkins Glen. Canal traffic peaked in 1854, but declined after the Civil War. The Chemung Canal was permanently closed in the winter of 1878. This view is near the present site of the Chemung Canal Trust Company.

The Red Jacket Garden restaurant in 1855, located on Carroll Street between Lake and Baldwin Streets, was Elmira's most exclusive restaurant of the mid-19th century. Owner William Lee sought and attracted Elmira's "best people." A small cover charge was assessed. The menu consisted of ice cream, non-alcoholic beverages, fruit, clams, and fresh Princess Bay Count Oysters, shipped daily from New York City. The yard had swings for the patrons' amusement. The Rev. Thomas K. Beecher is seen sitting at the left, legs crossed, at the table. Lee sold the restaurant in 1863, and, after many owners, it closed in 1881. The tall building in back is at the corner of Water and Baldwin Streets. This area is now covered by the Eastown Parking Garage.

This is Briggs Brewery on the Chemung Canal at East Second Street, c. 1870. Founded by Thomas Briggs in 1858 and sold to John Arnot Jr. in 1864, Briggs Brewery's specialty was India Pale Ale. In the 20th century, during prohibition, federal agents raided speakeasies and wildcat breweries. In 1927, 2,024 barrels of high-test beer were dumped into the Elmira sewers. In 1931, a raid uncovered 35,000 gallons of alcohol and two stills at the brewery. On April 22, 1933, during a raid at a warehouse on Canal Street, police and federal agents discovered an illegal alcohol pipeline from the Briggs Brewery through the city sewer system. Molasses was piped from Canal Street to the brewery, distilled, and alcohol was piped back through another line. It had an estimated capability of 5,000 gallons a day, and was one of the major illegal liquor suppliers on the East Coast.

The Deister family (brothers Jacob, Michael, John, and their families) came from Hesse-Darmstadt, Germany, in the 1850s. Jacob operated a butcher store at 763 East Church Street. Michael owned a saloon and restaurant at 322 East Church Street. John and his family operated a grocery at 801 East Church Street from 1867 to 1936. His grandson, William H. "Tax" Miller, carried on the family tradition. In this c. 1875 photo are, from left to right, John Deister Sr., John Jr., Mary (Riebel) Deister, Maude Deister, and Henry Deister.

This is the blacksmith shop of M. Dwight Palmer, located at 311 West Water Street. Palmer was born in 1843 in Elmira. During the Civil War, he enlisted with Company I, 141st New York volunteers, and marched with General Sherman. After the war, he became a blacksmith and lived with his wife, Fanny, and their children, Fannie and Harry, at 312 W. Water Street. Palmer died in 1890, but his business continued until about 1901. Behind the building, across the river, can be seen the Lewis Updyke Ice House at 460 Hudson Street. The year 1881 was Lewis's best year—the little snow produced the purest, clearest ice 20 inches thick.

Employees pose at the Bauman-Weyer Brickyard, located near Sullivan Street on Elmira's eastside. Clay from this spot was mixed with shale from the East Hill quarry (seen in the distance), formed, and then baked to make bricks for regional building construction. Clay excavations exposed a vein of water from nearby Newtown Creek which flooded the pit thereby closing the factory and creating Brick Pond. Ice houses replaced the brickyard. The brickyard moved to East Church Street and reformed as the Consolidated Brick Co. The central man in the dark suit in this picture is Edward A. Bauman, Brick Burner. He was born in Germany in 1851, lived at 957 Sullivan Street, and died in Elmira on April 16, 1909.

This is a view at the corner of Lake Street at Water Street, looking north. The first horse-pulled trolley line ran from Hanover Square, Horseheads, down Lake Road (the Elmira-Horseheads highway), onto Lake Street to Water Street, on Water to Main Street, on Main to Third Street, and on Third to Railroad Avenue (formerly Wisner Street). In 1871, cars ran every 15 minutes from 7 a.m. to 10 p.m. Fares were 5¢ within the city, 10¢ to 14th Street, and 15¢ to Horseheads. In 1890, electric cars took over. In 1939, Elmira converted to buses.

A panoramic view of Elmira in 1883 surveys downtown and eastern portions of our fair city. This photograph was taken from the Park Church tower. Note the bare hills in the background.

Herman J. Volbrecht was 23 years old when he emigrated from Germany in 1868. Herman was an excellent craftsman and partnered with other shoemakers before opening his own store at this location at 172 Lake Street and the corner of Market Street in 1878. Herman continued working until age 80, and he died in 1926. He and his wife, Katherine, lived at 708 East Water Street and had five children. His daughter, Barbara Volbrecht, owned Barbara's Trucking Company. The Michael Birmingham Saloon is seen next door at 170 Lake Street. These buildings were razed to make way for the original Steele Memorial Library, now the parking lot for Marine Midland Bank on Lake Street.

Pictured here are Mr. and Mrs. Benjamin Miller (at left) and Louis Lutz and his son J.J. (center in white aprons) in front of their businesses at 666 Dickinson Street at East Fifth Street. Mr. and Mrs. Miller ran the hotel and grocery. The Louis Lutz Meat Market was located here from 1881 to 1893 and then moved to Broadway on the southside. Louis Lutz emigrated from Waldsee, Germany, in 1881. J.J. Lutz later owned a meat market at 56 Pennsylvania Avenue. The building in this photo was used as apartments from around 1901 to 1965 and was razed in 1969.

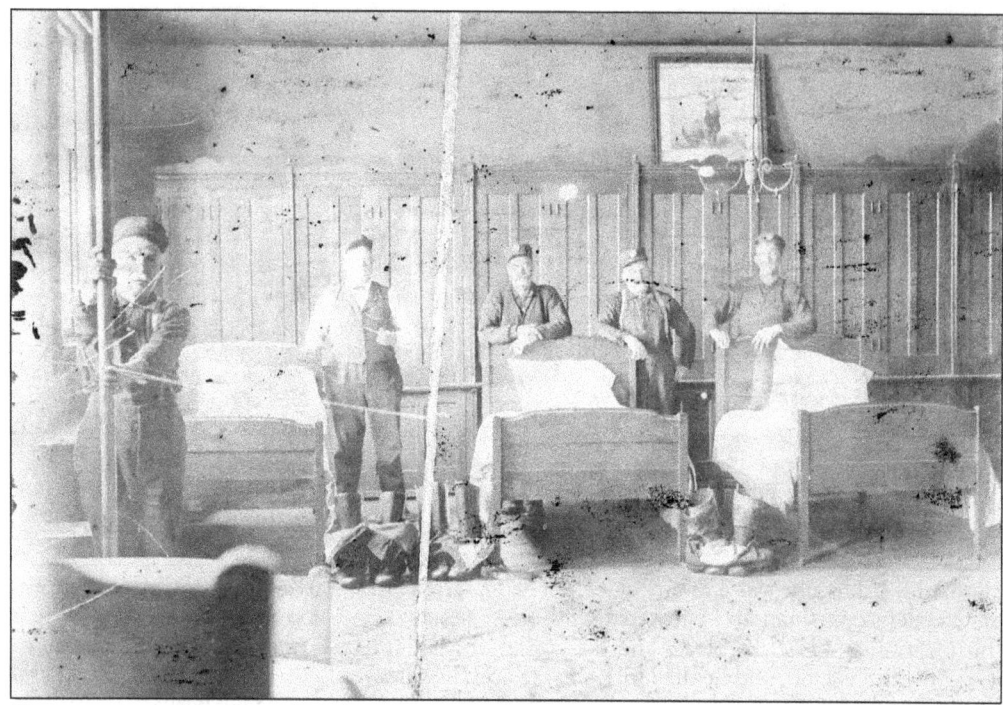

These men wait for a fire call at the Old Central Station on East Market Street, between the Owl Lunchroom and the Fred Jones Livery. From left to right are firefighters James O'Brien (residence at 727 Lake Street); Charles A. Hauenstein (residence at 217 Lormore Street); George Stevens; James Fay, a driver (residence at 710 Hatch Street); and Thomas "Malachi" O'Donnell, a driver (residence at 502 Roe Avenue). In 1998, the *Star Gazette* newspaper offices occupy this area.

During the Advertiser fire, fireman Charles Bentley was killed by a falling brick. William Naylor, a School of Commerce student, died in a stairway of the Robinson Building. Also lost in the fire was the Robinson Furniture store, Keatons Grocery, the *Sunday Tidings* newspaper, Suess Barber Shop, and the Bessey Laundry.

The caption on the reverse of this c. 1890 photo reads, "Uno—not forgotten." He worked at Hose Co. No. 1, Volunteer Firemen of Elmira.

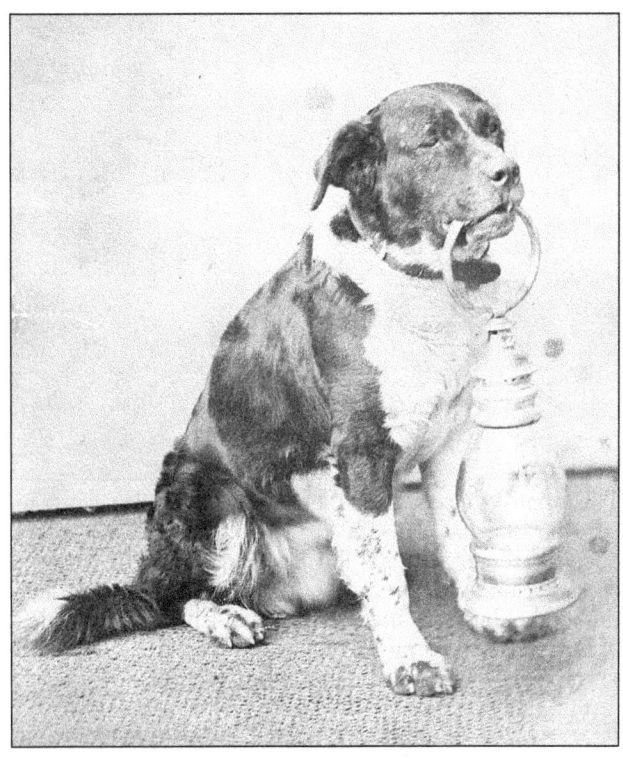

Firemen work to extinguish the devastating fire in the Advertiser and Robinson Buildings at Lake and Market Streets. The Advertiser Building caught fire at 7:50 p.m., February 15, 1888, while pressmen and printers were preparing the morning edition. Nine employees had to jump to a roof below the composing rooms. In the background is the Masonic Temple that would, itself, suffer a fire on March 23, 1914. The Masonic Temple building (with rebuilt top floor) serves today as Chemung County offices and courtroom.

This photo of a tobacco field near Fitch's Bridge was taken c. 1890. The peak tobacco growing years for Big Flats were 1908 to 1918, when 2,000 acres were planted. Five cigar rolling factories operated there. Lucinda and Ezra Fitch and their sons came to the region in the 1830s and built a beautiful house on the south side of the river, about 4 miles west of Elmira. Ezra was in the lumber business and was drowned while hauling a load of logs across the river with a team of horses. His sons raised money and constructed the first Fitch's Bridge. The Fitch brothers' sawmill was successful and profitable, clearing off a large farm and cutting more than 30 million feet of lumber.

In 1888, the Derby sisters, Cora and Eva, worked for Mr. Hosmer Billings' Book Store at 112 Baldwin Street. Eventually, it became the Derby Book Store. Shoppers were greeted with a personal atmosphere. The sisters recorded customers' heights on the door casing in the rear of the store. One of their tallest customers was Dr. H.A. Hamilton of Elmira College. You could also step on a scale to be weighed and recorded in a big book. Children were allowed to play on the ladders in the stacks to encourage their interest in books. On Saturday nights, the Salvation Army Band and Singers played outside the store. The store closed due to the 1946 flood. This building still stands opposite the Chemung Canal Bank on Baldwin Street.

"*It is a river that flows eastward, except when it leaves its banks and flows all over the town.*"

—Rudyard Kipling, a friend of Mark Twain,
while on a visit to Elmira in the summer of 1889.

This is a view of Water Street looking west from the corner of Baldwin Street; the photo was taken at 7:30 p.m. on June 1, 1889. The Chemung River rose nearly 21 feet above normal. Joe Benjamin, a candymaker known for his jokes and good humor, paddled a skiff into the Rathbun Hotel (on the corner of E. Water and Baldwin Streets) and asked for a room.

The 1889 flood was devastating, with home and business losses at over a quarter million dollars. This photo is at the corner of Madison and East Church Streets looking northeast.

This photo was made from the top of the Merchants Bank Building (107 West Water Street) looking west, during the 1889 flood. Curious and risk-taking Elmirans traverse the Main Street Bridge. The bridge, built in 1873, survived until 1920. The trees of Clinton Island can be seen in the middle of the river.

During the flood of 1889, the Erie Railroad Bridge was saved by parking fully loaded trains across the span. The water extended up Baldwin Street almost to Market Street. In 1934, the railroad tracks were raised to their present-day height.

This view of the damage caused on June 1, 1889, is looking east from the signal tracks tower at Pennsylvania Avenue. On the left in the distance is the American LaFrance building. The Fifth Ward (Elmira's southside) was almost completely under water.

This is the Old Buck House in Chemung, built in 1790, and the farm of Jesse Owen and son. The Buck family was important to the history of Chemung, New York, a town originally known as "Buckville." One of the Buck daughters married an Owen. Owen's Mills was founded when Harry and Jesse Owen built a mill there.

The Erie Railroad came to Elmira in 1849. By 1890, 2,500 Elmirans worked for Erie. Rick R. Dempsey was an engineer from 1885 to 1889 and lived at 364 Railroad Avenue. He worked for the Elmira *Telegram* in 1890; in 1891 he became a fireman, retiring in 1912. He moved to Addison in 1914.

Among those posing in this 1895 photograph is Constantine E. Bantley (upper right), owner of the Wire Works at the northwest corner of East Fifth Street at Madison Avenue. The company made iron, brass, and copper goods such as trellises, fences, and railings. They were in business from 1874 to about 1910. In 1998, this charming factory building still stands.

"The 1890s were exciting and progressive as the wonder of electric lighting and the telephone marched in step with the paving of dirt streets and the achievement of a pure water supply. Shops and small businesses rapidly multiplied to serve the needs of the growing population of Elmira."

—Thomas Byrne, Chemung County 1890–1975.

This view is looking east. Some stores of 1890 on West Water were Parmenter Hats at 118, West End Furniture at 116, Callahans Mens Clothing at 106, and Durland & Pratt Dry Goods & Carpets at 102.

In this view of Lake Street, looking north from Water Street c. 1890, street cars were the main form of transportation. This car was part of the Maple Avenue Railway. William H. Frost Jewelry at 335 East Water Street started there in 1886. William lived at 700 E. Church Street.

Joseph Meyer's Drug Store was at the southeast corner of Lake and Water Streets. Joseph Meyer (left) lived at 756 East Water Street. Peter J. Lutz (right) was born in Waldsee, Germany, and came to Elmira with his family in 1871. He studied and qualified for the drug business, and, in 1891, he formed a partnership with F.X. Kaster and started a German pharmacy at 531 Lake Street.

"One wouldn't think of picnicking at Eldridge unless the linen tablecloth was all newly ironed and fresh linen napkins rolled and standing in the drinking glasses . . . 2 bouquets of flowers, and fancy china plates."

—Mabel Cramer Wood.

This family picnic at Eldridge Park took place c. 1890. The man standing is Charles "Charlie" Lovell (1872–1953) at age 18. He had a store at Pigeon Point in 1900, and in 1905 he opened "Lovell's" across the street at 1131 Lake Street, a landmark that became dear to the hearts of generations of Elmirans for its Giant Sodas and Lucky Mondays. Charlie was an excellent amateur photographer, and some of his scenes of old Elmira are in the collection of the Chemung County Historical Society. His home was at 305 E. Clinton. When he retired in 1952, he was Elmira's oldest living pharmacist. The man and woman in dark clothes (seated) are Mr. and Mrs. Aaron Cramer of 1304 Pratt Street.

The Chemung River is pictured here looking west from the Main Street Bridge.

The 30th Separate Company marches down North Main Street on July 22, 1892. On the left is the W.H. Ross Grocery, and on the right is the John C. Diehl Bakery, George Rogers Grocery, and the Hooker and Dorr Drugstore. St. Patrick's spire can be seen in the background. Note the boys in the fountain and early street lighting (see p. 125).

Arcalous Welling Wyckoff founded the A. Wyckoff & Son Wood Pipe Manufactory in 1855. The company made wooden pipes and other products with their patented boring machine, invented by Elmiran Lafayette Stevens. Thousands of farmers bought Wyckoff Chain Pumps, which were housed in classic wooden frames with a crank on the side. The factory was originally located on Chemung Place and then moved to 100–108 Home Street. Wyckoff closed in 1945. The Chemung Place factory was located near the southern approach of the Clemens Center Parkway Bridge.

This is the John T. Ayers Carriage Factory (1868–1915), located on College Avenue at Third Street. Mr. Ayers produced fine handcrafted carriages. He and his family lived at 408 College Avenue. The building still stands and is occupied by the Garrick's College & Third tavern.

Samuel H. Laney began his business career in 1872 by peddling rags and raising chickens. By 1874, he sold everything—wrapping paper, rubber goods, tinware, earthenware, glassware, stoves, beds, rags, and second-hand items. S.H. Laney Rag & Paper Dealer had several warehouses, located at 151, 605, and 657 (this photo) Baldwin Street, and an office at Market and William Streets. Samuel was in business from around 1874 to 1895. This photo, taken c. 1880, shows Baldwin Street looking north. In 1998, the houses on the right are the site of the John Jones Court Housing Complex.

We are looking south on Baldwin Street from Market in this c. 1891 photograph. On the extreme left is McConnell's Rialto Music Hall at 160 Baldwin Street. Next on the left is Manning R. Roll's Artists' Supplies. At the end of the street is M.A. Ruger, Jeweler. The big building on the right is the Rathbun Hotel. On the extreme right is A.T. Rice Seeds and Flowers at 165 Baldwin Street.

D.W. Seely owned the Elephant Billiard Parlor at 160 Lake Street, seen in this c. 1893 photo. Marine Midland Bank on Lake Street now occupies this space.

In 1893, Albert Vickery's The Fair was located at 134 West Water Street. It is believed to be the first 5 and 10 cent store in Elmira. Albert was in business from 1874 to 1898; he then became secretary for the Columbia Gold Mining Company in Elmira. His home was at 218 Washington Street.

The Fritsch Grocery at West Fourteenth Street and College Avenue opened in 1894. Charles and Catherine Fritsch stand outside with their children, August and Harold. Harold took over the store about 1920. By 1928, Harold had sold the store and worked for McCorkle Real Estate. The sign on building reads, "Park Coal Yard." Samples of coal are in front of the store, and the coal sizes in the box are "Egg-Stove-Nut-Pea." Orders for coal were taken here. The building still stands at 120 W. Fourteenth. Over the years, the building has served as restaurants under different names.

Grocers Charles and Catherine Fritsch are seen here inside their store in 1894.

The Kanaweola Cycling Club stops for a pose in front of the Elmira Reformatory on July 4, 1895. Originally a club for men, it had its start in the 1860s. They went on tours and day trips to Watkins Glen, Big Flats, Corning, Pine City, Millport, Caton, etc. They even had a small indoor track in the Steele Memorial Library Building to use when the weather was bad. The name Kanaweola has been spelled in various ways. The word was a Seneca Indian name for the Indian village at the junction of Newtown Creek and the Chemung River and means "head on a pole."

Good food was always served at Richard D. Baltz's Eating House at 319 Carroll Street, seen here in 1895. Richard (left) was 59 years old at this time, and he retired before 1900. Fridie Dry Cleaners claimed this building in 1946. In 1955, it was part of C&K Cleaners. In 1998, it is under the Eastowne Parking Garage.

The 99 Cent Store was in business from about 1891 to 1910. It was located at 112 West Water Street and owned by Charles Lantaff (left), who lived across the street at the Wyckhoff House at 117 West Water Street. Charles's brother William ran a 5 & 10 a few doors up the street.

Thomas Lawrence's Candy Store operated from 1878 to 1900 at 138 West Water Street. Although Thomas's specialty was chocolate, he was also well known for his butter creams. Currently, this location is occupied by the Club Nautilus Fitness Center.

The Commercial Hotel was operated by T. McCarthy Fennell and his wife, Margaret Mary, both of County Clare, Ireland. T. McCarthy fought in the Fenian Rebellion in Ireland, was wounded in the Battle of Killklooney Wood, and was captured and exiled for life in prison to Australia in 1867. Margaret Mary never expected to see him again and came to America with his brother's family in 1871. At about the same time ,T. McCarthy and several prisoners escaped from prison and he joined Margaret Mary in Elmira. In 1874, he ran the Tioga Hotel at 603 Railroad Avenue. In 1876, he ran a saloon at 507 Railroad Avenue. Eventually, he ran the Commercial Hotel at 601 Railroad Avenue, and, by 1912, he was also operating a travel agency specializing in ocean cruises. The Fennells had three exceptional children—all graduated college. Matthias was an Elmira dentist, Mary graduated from Elmira College and was a teacher at Elmira Free Academy, and Thomas Jr. was an Elmira lawyer and, later, a judge. Their home was at 416 W. Clinton Street. Mr. Fennell died around 1913.

In 1895, George M. Hollister and George Hyatt operated a horseshoeing business at the northwest corner of State and Gray Streets, where the post office is now. Hollister lived at 910 John Street; Hyatt lived at 222 Gregg Street.

The Gleason Health Resort was established in 1852 by Dr. Silas O. Gleason and Dr. Rachel Brooks Gleason. Both were pioneers in the treatment of diseases by water (mineral baths) and other natural remedies. When the Gleasons retired, the hospital went to Dr. John Fisher. The Watercure Hill sanitarium continued and later became a nursing home. It was razed in 1959. All that remains is a stone pillar at the entrance to the drive on Watercure Hill Road.

Pictured here are students at Elmira School #3 at 113 East Hudson Street in the former building of the Elmira Surgical Institute (now the area of Tops Supermarket on Elmira's southside). The school moved to Mt. Zoar Street and was renamed for an important educator, Parley Coburn. In 1890, the school census of Elmira showed a total of 7,968 children of school age, 4,413 in public schools, 760 in private schools, and 2,795 not attending school.

This photograph of East Water Street, looking west from Lake Street, was taken c. 1895. The Frost Building is on the right at 335 East Water Street. Elmira mayor and lawyer Edgar Denton had an office on the second floor. The Queen City had a busy retail area. Naptha lighting came in the 1870s. In 1885, sidewalks were made of hemlock planks. Gaslights came in 1892. By 1894, the streets were paved with bricks. Downtown drew customers from a market much greater than the Chemung County region.

A horse-drawn ambulance waits at the front door of Arnot-Ogden Hospital around 1895. The hospital was opened in 1888.

The first telephone directory listed 42 Elmirans with telephones. This office in 1896 was at the corner of State and Nicks Streets (now the parking lot of the Chemung Canal Bank). Pictured, from left to right, are Sylvia Gleason, Jennie DeGroff, Winifred Drake, Gertrude Bertell, Helen Meade, Libbie Murray, May Rutan, Winifred Sadler, Grace LeShear, Augusta Rockwell, manager F. Eugene Smith (residence was 421 W. Clinton), Bertha Graner, and Myrtle Beckhorn. At the desk in foreground is Kittie Butcher (residence was 206 Dewitt Street).

This 1895 snowy scene in old Elmira was made by Charles Lovell, a pharmacist and ice-cream man.

The West End Hotel was in business from 1880 to 1926 at 232–234 West Water Street. The photo was taken c. 1895. Next door on the left is the William Carpenter Livery. This area is occupied in 1998 by the mirrored building in the block between College and Main.

Baldwin Kolb (the big man behind the bar) ran the Queen City Palace Hotel at 117 Lake Street after 1880. He had been in the saloon business since 1866 with his brother Jacob at the Exchange Hotel, and in 1876 at the Kolb and Snyder Saloon at 338–40 East Water Street. Baldwin retired around 1908; his home was at 118 College Avenue. Jacob continued at the Exchange Hotel until he became the city tax assessor; his home was at 616 North Main Street. The man sitting at the table is William F. Maurer, who eventually bought this saloon from Kolb. He later owned William Maurer's Saloon at 140 East Water Street around 1900. The Queen City Palace Hotel occupied the space that is now the exit ramp for the Eastowne Parking Garage.

Elmirans naturally headed west along the banks of the Chemung to enjoy good weather and weekends. Roricks Glen, Senators Cottage, and Clarks Glen were favorite stops along the Elmira, Corning, and Waverly (EC&W) Rail Line. Pictured here is the Fisk Restaurant in 1898, just above Fitch's Bridge. Chicken dinners were 50¢.

On February 18, 1899, the Cotton Brothers Moving Company hoisted the county's treasury safe through a second-floor window at the county buildings on the Market Street side. The moving of safes was a specialty of the Cotton brothers (George and Sam). Their first office was across the street from the Howell Box Factory on the southside. A large shed that is still there marks the old Cotton staging area. The Cottons were in business from 1874 until after 1917. At their peak, they had 14 wagons for general and specialized hauling.

The original Steele Memorial Library opened on August 2, 1899, at the southeast corner of Lake and Market Streets, next door to Friend, Metzger & Co. Mrs. Esther Baker Steele donated this building as a memorial to her husband, Dr. Joel Dorman Steele. She put aside a portion of her annual income until enough money had accumulated for such a project, and planned for the building to have rental office spaces to support the existence of the library—a plan that worked in other communities, but failed in Elmira. Deficits occurred annually beginning in the first year and continuing until 1921, when the Carnegie Corporation gave the generous gift of a new library, which was to be built at the southeast corner of Lake and Church Streets.

Clinton Island provided popular summer relief for Elmirans in the 19th and early 20th centuries. It was a retreat for parties of pleasure, swimming, boating, picnics, and romantic walks. People could get to the island by using the wooden stairs from the Lake and Walnut Street Bridges. Clinton Island was stripped of its greenery in the 1946 flood.

The cool river breezes were the perfect respite on a hot July afternoon. The latest swimsuit fashions, ice cream, and hand holding were part of the fun.

On the bridge at Beckwith Farm are, from left to right, unknown, Mrs. Geer, Margaret Geer (a telephone operator), Elmer Geer (a template maker at the Bridgeworks who resided at 561 Thompson Street), Lester Geer, Albert Beam (a worker at the Bridgeworks who resided at 523 Penn), Clarence Beam (eventually a worker for Penn Railroad), Florence Beam (a clerk at the telephone company), and Mrs. Albert Beam.

The footbridge to the Capt. Daniel G. Beckwith Farm on Big Island, east of the foot of Cedar Street at Maple Avenue, is seen here. Captain Beckwith fought at Bull Run and Fredericksburg. He was shot, and his leg was amputated. He was a successful farmer who was elected town clerk (two terms) and justice of the peace (five terms).

West Side Railroad car #19 and a double-deck trailer on West Side Avenue at the Erie Depot at Eldridge Park are seen in this photograph made by Van Aken Studios in the summer of 1893.

On the reverse of this c. 1900 photo, it says, "Jim Creighton—on top left with co-workers and trolley line truck in Elmira Heights. The Collie dog [far right] always followed the wagon." James F. Creighton was a motorman and lived at 1851 Davis Street. In September 1896, the first Oakwood Methodist Church was dedicated; its spire is visible past the pole. The building on the left currently houses Heights Laundry.

This is the golf course at the Elmira Country Club, c. 1915, and the first clubhouse can be seen on the hill. The present clubhouse was built in 1920 after the land was purchased from the John Hendy Farm site. Considered the founder of the club, J. Sloat Fassett, noted in business and politics, discovered golf during a visit to Scotland in the 1890s. Among the rules of 1897 was this one: "All balls found on the ground are the property of the club." Caddies were paid 10¢ an hour (see p. 75).

Eldridge Lake was a popular site for boating, picnicking, romantic strolls, and summer evening fireworks displays. In its heyday, Elmirans felt that Eldridge Park, with its shimmering lake, graceful statues, shaded walkways, and cozy picnic grounds, rivaled New York City's Central Park.

Pictured here are rowboats in the Chemung River at the Pine Cliffs Club at Bohemia, west of Fitch's Bridge in 1902.

The theatrical heyday at Rorick's Glen was from 1900 to 1918. Rorick's had a 1,200-seat open-air auditorium. Many excellent performances were given by nationally and locally known talent, such as the Manhattan Opera Company, the Frank Hauver Band, and the Trinity Church Choir. Vivian Vance and Edward Everett Horton were also in several stage plays here. Snow and rain-making machines added interest to the productions. Families dined before the show on the spacious lawns and picnic grounds.

Two
TURN OF THE CENTURY

This photo shows East Water Street at State Street (looking east) being modernized, c. 1901. The laying and repairing of trolley tracks was an extremely difficult job. The bricks had to be removed and replaced after the new tracks were installed. Some of the stores shown here with East Water Street addresses are K. Barnett Milliner, Dr. George Merrill, and the Elmira Savings Bank at 126 (now the southwest corner of Water Street and the Clemens Center Parkway); Mrs. Walsh's Millinery parlor at 130; Louis Shidlein's Saloon at 132; C. Feigenstein's and Peter P. Conroy at 202; Cole and Matthews at 135; Reynold's Brothers and Warnock's at 137; and Rosenbaum & Sons at 201. Nearly all of the pictured buildings have been razed since the 1972 flood.

The *Telegram*, Elmira's first Sunday newspaper, began on May 7, 1879. It filled the news gap by reporting weekend news. The business was started by Elmirans Charles Hazard, Henry Brooks, and James Hill, with venture capital of $25 apiece (two of the three men had to borrow their $25). For decades, it was the best-selling newspaper between New York City and Buffalo. The paper's mascot was named "Colonel," and he was "the finest St. Bernard Dog on earth." A fire destroyed the newspaper building, at the corner of Exchange and Market Streets, on March 13, 1913 (see p. 74).

The cornerstone for the post office was set on the corner of E. Church Street and State Street. The post office officially opened on September 13, 1903, with walls of Vermont marble, oak, woodwork, and a marble staircase. The price tag was $275,000.

Miss Kingston's kindergarten class is seen here at School #1 (now known as Thomas K. Beecher School) on Sullivan Street near East Church. Previously this was the location of a one-room schoolhouse. The date of this picture is unknown.

Graduation day finally arrived for these anxious students of Old School #4. Miss Brooks (third row, second from left) was the principal. Built in 1875, the school was located at Division and Hall Streets until it was razed and replaced with a new school named for George M. Diven in 1930.

This young woman was the champion of Rufus Stanley's Bread Making Club. All of his clubs' champions were awarded exciting field trips to places like Washington and New York. Other clubs included the Handicraft Club, the Rural School Club, the Corn Club, and the Poultry Raising Club. The Omega Club supported all forms of farm work. Eventually, Stanley consolidated all the clubs into the Achievement Club, a forerunner of the 4-H programs in Chemung County.

This is Rufus Stanley's Rambling Club at Quarry Farm, the summer home to Samuel Clemens and his family. "Ellerslie" was a playhouse for Clemens's children. The Fotographic Rambling Club was a hiking club for young photographers. Stanley introduced members to the natural beauty of our region by using photography as a means to observe. In their ramblings, the group went to Quarry Farm, the Watercure, Watkins Glen, and Rorick's Glen. Photos from this club represent some of the finest among the Chemung Valley History Museum's collection.

Rufus Stanley (1859–1926) was always interested in the betterment of people. Raised in a Christian home, it was his desire to help mankind from a very young age. Stanley worked briefly at the Elmira Reformatory to study the "start of crime." He consulted frequently with Superintendent Zebulon Brockway and interviewed the inmates. In his mind, Stanley formulated and developed programs that promoted a "sound body and a sound mind."

Rufus Stanley founded a variety of clubs for men, women, and children. The Night Walkers Club was for older boys and men who wanted to go on evening walks to the East Hill quarry or some similar location, cook their suppers over an outdoor fire, sing songs, and tell stories.

Morale was high among the Willys-Morrow employees. Besides a band, there were also the Willys-Morrow baseball league, Wednesday night movies, a glee club, and dances.

The First Baptist Church of Elmira has had three churches on its property adjoining Wisner Park. In 1830, the first church was erected. By 1849, the congregation had outgrown that church and built a bigger one. The third and present building was constructed in 1892. The trolley cars ran Sunday mornings to take people to church.

This view of the flood on Carroll Street looking east toward Madison Avenue was taken on March 1, 1902. On the left are Andrew O'Dea, Blacksmith, at 431 Carroll, and Orris Danks Feed & Seed at 433. On the right are Welsh Hack Stable, owned by James H. Morrisey at 432, and Scientific Food, J.S. Fassett, president, at 434. At the end of street is the old German church, now known as the First United Church of Christ.

This July 1902 photo shows the temporary bridge to Rorick's Glen amusement area that was built after that year's damaging flood. Note the trolley circle and refreshment stands on the opposite shore. Corn and tobacco fields and barns would soon give way to suburban development.

Frederick V. Ensign was a manufacturer of display hooks, metal goods, novelties, and hair pins, etc. His business was located at 428–432 Erie Street, near the corner of Falck Street. This photograph was taken c. 1910.

Employees pose in the yard at the Erie Railroad.

This was William H. "Tax" Miller's Meat Market at 561 East Water Street near Melvin Street, c. 1899. In 1905, Miller was working at Friend-Metzger. In 1907, he took charge of the Lyceum Cafe at 156 Lake Street (see p. 67). William's maternal grandfather, John Deister, arrived in Elmira from Germany in 1855 and operated a grocery on East Church Street (see p. 12). William was born in 1873, the son of Jacob and Abbie (Deister) Miller, and lived at his boyhood home, 616 Jay Street, for almost his entire life. One of his first jobs was at the Wire Works on East Fifth Street. William's young wife, Minnie, and infant son, William Jr., died in 1908. Their daughter Grace was a beloved English teacher at Elmira Free Academy from 1928 to 1966.

Friend-Metzger was an old-country German butcher shop opened in 1864 by John Friend at 164–66 Lake Street. It was located in the block that is now the Marine Midland Bank on Lake Street. In this c. 1905 photo, William H. "Tax" Miller is at the scales.

Mailman John Brockway delivers mail on his rural route in 1903.

A delivery wagon from John Brand & Co. sits in front of the Howell Box Factory. John Brand Sr. established a leaf tobacco business in 1873 with a tobacco plantation in the Buttonwoods area of the southside and an office on the northside. After his father's death, John Brand Jr. moved the office from Fourth Street and Railroad Avenue to the south approach of the Lake Street Bridge. Besides growing his own tobacco, Brand also imported tobacco from Havana. The business declined in the early 1900s as cigarettes grew in popularity and closed in 1927. Howell was their primary supplier of cigar boxes. The Brand shop and warehouse still remain as Howell Liberatore and Associates.

Two young women stroll down Lake Street at the turn of the century. The building in the left background is the Arnot family home, now the Arnot Art Museum. The iron fence was recycled for war efforts.

Mr. William C. Hall worked at the Elmira Beef Company until his death at age 42 in 1903. Pictured here, from right to left, are his wife, Mrs. Mahala Hall, and their two daughters, Edna and Eva, shortly after his death. Their home was at 516 High Street. Currently, this house is still in use.

Herbert Snyder enjoys a canoe trip in the summer of 1904. At this time, Herb was a clerk for Timothy S. Pratt, a home furnishings dealer at 311 East Water Street (see p. 71).

On its way to Corning, the Elmira, Corning, and Waverly Railroad Trolley car #109 was derailed by a landslide above the Narrows Road (now Route 352).

This photograph of the midway at the Chemung County Fair was taken c. 1903. The fair has been a showcase for agriculture and showbusiness since 1842. Elmira hosted seven state fairs until Syracuse was chosen as the official site. The fairgrounds were originally at the site of the Kennedy Valve on the eastside, then near Dunn Field on the southside, and finally, in 1892, at its present location north of the city in Horseheads.

This is a view of Main Street looking north from Water Street. All the trolley lines in Elmira branched out from this point. In 1904, Thomas Routledge moved his jewelry store from Pigeon Point to Water and Main Streets. The Werdenbergs store on the left survived in business at this location for nearly a century. Many of these buildings are still in use.

Mary Dove is seen here at her home at 1124 Walnut Street, c. 1905. She was the first baker at the Elmira Reformatory. Mary was the widow of George Dove. This house was located just outside the present entrance to Woodlawn Cemetery.

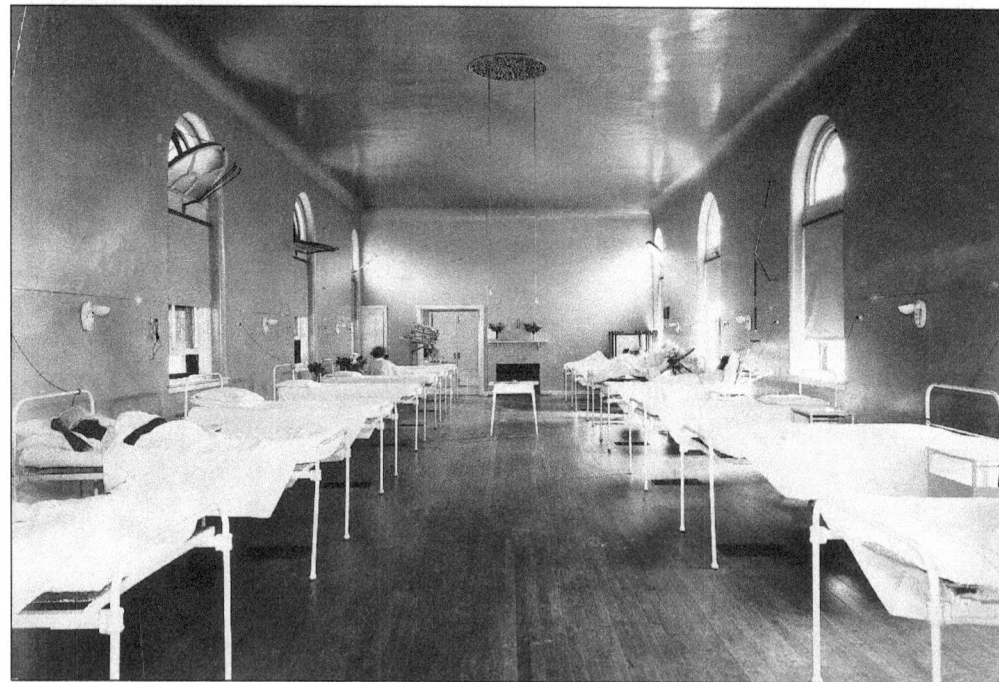

One of the wards in the original wings of the Arnot-Ogden Hospital is pictured here around 1904. In 1889, the hospital's first full year of operation, 97 patients were admitted.

Looking north on State Street in 1905, the telephone pole marks the corner of Gray Street. The tall dark building on the right was John M. Connelly Liquors at 258–60 State Street. In the distance is Elmira Storage and Supply at the northwest corner of Church and State Streets. Some of old State Street still exists, but most of it has been incorporated into the Clemens Center Parkway. The Connelly Building still stands and is occupied by A-1 Printing and Jerry Laughlin Insurance. (Photo by Frank Ridall.)

William D. Reid's Birds and Fishes, a pet store and taxidermist at 204 Baldwin Street (at Market Street), was in business here from 1889 to 1917. The tall man (third from the right) is Charles Schiller. Charles was a housepainter who lived at 857 East Market Street. Shown here c. 1905, the site is the present location of the office of the New York State Department of Labor.

Rorick's Glen was the amusement place for Elmirans at the beginning of the 20th century. Over the course of its history, the area offered hiking trails, burro rides, music, dancing, and mechanical rides. The Roricks open-air playhouse was one of the finest in the United States and featured vaudeville, minstrel shows, and the Manhattan Opera Company. Summer performances were jammed nightly. Rorick's Glen had a strict rule of "No alcohol." This photo of the concession stand was taken c. 1905.

Pleasure seekers in the early years of the 20th century traveled to Rorick's Glen via the West Water Street trolley for 5¢. A trolley spurline ended on the northside of the river where patrons then walked across the wooden bridge. Margaret Curren (the great aunt of author Diane L. Janowski) says the swing in the foreground was fun and exciting, especially when it swung you out over the river at night. This view is from 1910 looking northwest.

At the turn of the century, Mr. and Mrs. John P. Frantz owned and operated a water toboggan near Fitch's Bridge, west of Elmira. They offered a refreshment stand and bathing suit rentals. Mrs. Frantz's rule was "Only persons in bathing suits are permitted to take the plunge into the river." This photo is dated 1906.

Pine City artist Lars Hoftrup sketches the river, c. 1908.

In 1910, the Edward Kaier Grocery was located at 561 East Second Street (now a vacant lot) at the corner of High Street. German-born Edward and his wife, Amelia, ran the grocery from 1876 to 1913. Kaier then sold it to the Algeier family and Timothy Rhodes.

This photograph of a music class at the Neighborhood House was taken c. 1905 (see p. 90).

Elisha Van Aken and his son, Charles Van Aken, served Elmirans for 60 years as the region's most accomplished portrait and landscape photographers. This view of the Buttonwoods was made by Charles, c. 1906. The Buttonwoods area near Brand Park (from Maple Avenue east to the river) was named for the large Buttonwood or sycamore trees that still grow there.

Founded in 1889, Elmira Bridge was the forerunner of the American Bridge Company. The original plant was located on Erie Street on Elmira's southside. Operations moved permanently to the Elmira Heights location in 1900. Among the projects completed here were the Sixth Avenue Elevated in New York, part of the Chicago Elevated, and the Walnut Street, Lake Street, and Madison Avenue Bridges in Elmira.

Daniel Kennedy was encouraged to move his manufacturing facility from Coxsackie, New York, to Elmira by John M. Connelly and Fred LeValley in 1907. The foundry is well known for fire hydrants and automatic sprinklers.

This is the interior of the passenger car of the Glen Route Trolley. The Glen Route was one of the earliest inter-urban electric railways built in New York state and one of the first to be abandoned. The trolley's first trip was on May 19, 1900. It ran every half hour from 6 a.m. to 11:30 p.m., and its 22-mile route took 90 minutes. Service ended on November 11, 1923.

"For a weekend trip this outing appeals to the whole family. For the head of the family this trip offers splendid diversion. He can relieve his wife of the responsibilities of household duties by taking the whole family for a ride over the Glen Route line to Watkins Glen and everyone will come back greatly rested and benefited."

—Elmira *Advertiser* advertisement, 1908.

Pictured here is a Glen Route trolley at its regular stop in Millport, NY. The line began at the Rathbun Hotel and traveled east on Water Street to Lake Street, north on Lake Street to Hanover Square in Horseheads, and then to downtown Watkins Glen.

Willis Friends of Mt. Zoar Hill sold wagons for Myer H. Friendly's carriage business. In this photo, Willis is starting a trip to sell buggies. His home was at 218 High Street. Myer Friendly began selling saddlery and hardware in 1874. His carriage showroom was at 102–104 State Street (presently the parking lot of the Chemung Canal Bank), and he lived at 510 W. Church Street, now the Glove House. (Photo by Arthamese Denny.)

Milkman Howard Bowen of Elmira Heights was in business from about 1901 to 1917 at Oakwood and Sixteenth Streets. His slogan was "Just Milk." Once a horse knew a delivery route, it could travel without much direction from the driver.

On their way to a parade, c. 1918, the three men in car are, from left to right, Grant DeVed (who managed the Rathbun House Hotel and died in his room in September 1929), Frank Carroll (a traveling salesman who lived at 616 W. First Street), and William H. "Tax" Miller (a butcher and cafe owner, also pictured in the photograph below). The Rathbun House was modeled after New York City's Murray Hill Hotel. It had a high-ceilinged dining room, a big lobby with marble columns, leather chairs, a famous bar, and a billiard room. "Everything was big, restful, unhurried, and gracious."

The Lyceum Cafe at 156 Lake Street was famous for its delicious turkey sandwiches. William H. "Tax" Miller, a friendly host, operated the Lyceum Cafe (next to the Lyceum Theatre) from 1907 in partnership with his uncle, Jacob Riebel. Their clientele included stars of vaudeville and the silent screen. The theatre eventually closed and, with it, the cafe. On his own, William opened the Beaux Arts Cafe nearby on Carroll Street and worked there until his death on January 20, 1929. The Beaux Arts continued until at least 1950 (see p. 53).

This is a 1911 view of the valley of the Chemung River from Sullivan's Monument.

Sullivan's Monument was erected for the centennial anniversary celebration of the Battle of Newtown and was dedicated on August 29, 1879. The material used in its construction was not of a character that would insure its permanency. Eleven years later, the monument had crumbled, and it finally collapsed during a storm on August 30, 1911. The new and present monument was erected in 1912.

This c. 1910 photograph shows Water Street looking east toward Main Street after a good snow.

Henry Crummel Washington (on left) started barbering in 1872 and opened his own shop at 424 East Water Street. He retired in 1918 and became a janitor for the Elmira *Advertiser*. Henry's mother-in-law was Mrs. Mary Cord, Samuel Clemens's cook at Quarry Farm. The Clemens family called her "Aunty Cord." Sam said she was "very tall, very broad, and very fine." Sometimes Aunty Cord took Henry's seven children to work with her so they could play with the Clemens children.

The Elmira Automobile Club's road signs were the first to be put up to help drivers navigate the region. Here, with his car, is M.R. Ellis, secretary of the club in 1912.

June 9, 1911, was an exciting day in Southport, when the Elmira Water, Light and Railroad Company extended their trolley line from Miller Street to Southport Corners. In the "Golden Spike" celebration, Mrs. Mamie Sheely hit the spike with the ceremonial hammer (see p. 87). The lawn of the South Presbyterian Church (now the Southport Baptist Church) was used for the festivities. The photo shows Southport Street, Caton Avenue, and Pennsylvania Avenue. At this ceremony, Southport was predicted to become the most "beautiful suburb."

On June 25, 1911, Herbert Snyder takes a photo looking downstream from the Rorick's Glen Bridge. Herbert was employed by the Sheehan, Dean Co. and lived at 722 Columbia Street (see p. 56).

Seasonal recreation for Elmirans is seen here, c. 1912. Canoes were rented from Bill Cotton's Canoe Livery at 311 W. Water Street and taken to Gibson on EC&W Railroad flat cars. From there, boaters leisurely paddled back to downtown Elmira.

"Independent Hose Co. No. 3," located at the intersection of Pennsylvania Avenue and South Main Street, is seen in this c. 1900 photograph. Seated on the right is John C. Espey, who was appointed chief of the Elmira Fire Department in 1904. Dan Kane is holding the reins. At the firehouse, the harness was suspended from the ceiling so it could be dropped quickly on the horses. When a modern fire station was constructed on Miller Street, this building was razed (see p. 121, top).

Ernest W. Goodrich (barber on left) of 357 Pomeroy Place was the uncle of Joseph A. Blash (barber on right) of 369 W. Second Street. They were partners from about 1910 to 1914 at 101 State Street. Joseph continued barbering, while Ernest became an insurance agent. The building at 101 State Street was razed in 1938. It is currently the site of WETM-TV.

"The best beer in the state is coming from the Mander's Brewery at the foot of East Church Street. The business was started in 1857 by Adam Mander. There are storage vaults 50 feet underground filled with the season's supply . . . malt and storage rooms 3 stories high . . . and the brewery 2 stories high."

—Elmira *Daily Advertiser*, May 10, 1883.

In this 1911 photo are, from left to right, John Deister, Henry Mander, Fred Myers, George Mander, August Ross, Will Ewald, Harry (Hartley H.) Geddes, and Frank G. Belo. The beer cellars were cut into the solid rock at the base of East Hill and were later expanded to form the Church Street exit ramp from Route 17.

Church and State Streets are the focus of this *c.* 1911 photograph. The new post office (extreme right) opened in 1903. North on State Street, Henry Heine and Edward Bauer ran an upholstery business and, beyond that, is the Charles M. and Ray Tompkins Building, built in 1887. The Tompkins Company was the first in Elmira to import tea. Tompkins had a separate building for roasting, grinding, and packaging their own brand of coffee, Sancuta, which boasted it had "more caffeine than any other coffee." The building of Frank H. Allen, a painter, stands where the YMCA building is now. The Tompkins Co. Building is now occupied by the Coon Heating & Manufacturing Co.

The south side of West Water Street, west of Main, is seen here in the middle of winter, 1912. On the left is the Alice Frances Hotel at 201–205 West Water, Harris the Hatman at 207, Wing Lee's Laundry at 209, and A.B. Colony Bicycles at 211.

The Elmira Telegram fire is seen here from Water Street on the evening of March 13, 1913. The newspaper was located at the corner of Market and Exchange Streets near the present Nixon Building (see p. 46).

A mechanical class at the Vocational School (Old School #6), located at 717–21 Lake Street, is shown here. This was a special school for elementary students who were "not remotely interested in the offerings of typical schools," according to Thomas Byrne in *Chemung County 1890–1975*. The school was open from 1914 to 1924 and was closed when vocational courses were added to the curriculum at the new Southside High School.

Nurses stand at the wide-open windows of Elmira's Tuberculosis Sanitarium. The first tuberculosis sanitarium was opened in 1910 in the building at the top of Underwood Avenue, which was formerly the Elmira Country Club House. The first building burned in 1915 and was replaced in 1917. The facility was discontinued in 1955, and patients were transferred to an Ithaca hospital. Tuberculosis treatment in 1910 cost $12 per week for local residents, $14 for out of towners, and was free if you could not afford to pay. Treatment consisted of bed rest and breathing fresh crisp air (see p. 43).

Lincoln Beachey, the leading stunt pilot in the United States from 1911 to 1914, performs his "Championship of the Universe" show at the Maple Avenue Driving Park. Beachey, in a Curtiss Biplane, raced a Chalmers 40 automobile sponsored by the LaFrance Motor Car Company. The auto was driven by George Saulsman. The plane above and the auto below left the mark at the same time, but, when the three laps had ended, Beachey had gained a lap. Stores and factories closed to allow employees to see the excitement (which took place just west of present-day Dunn Field). Ten thousand people attended the July 1912 event. Beachey's specialty was his "death dive." While performing this stunt on March 14, 1915, in his hometown, both wings broke off his Martin monoplane, and he fell to his death in San Francisco Bay. (Photo by Frank Ridall.)

The Elmira Moose Lodge Women's Auxiliary Band always enjoyed a good parade. Moose Lodge charities supported the Child City, a retirement center in Mooseheart, Illinois, and Moose Haven, Florida.

Pictured here are four friends and employees at the Louis A. Corning Ice Cream Company, located at 411–415 W. Second Street from 1910 to 1919. From left to right, they are as follows: (seated) Earl Ferguson, Roland Corning (a student living at 520 W. Third Street), and Will P. Hinds (who in 1919 became a coach cleaner for the Pennsylvania Railroad and lived at 362 Columbia Street); (standing) Charles A. Mitchell (a student who became a collector for New York Telephone and lived at 666 Beecher Street).

In 1915, sisters Elsie Cleveland Marinan and Mary Cleveland operated the Bon Ton Tea Room on the second floor of 323 East Water Street, over the Terbell-Calkins Drug Store.

On June 24, 1916, Company L of Elmira posed in uniform on Church Street. Five thousand people from Chemung County served in World War I. Note that several of the buildings remain to this day, including the old post office, the old Century Club, and the LeValley

During World War I, Elmira College students had a Victory Garden. In this 1918 photo, the "Farmerettes" keep their onions growing in their garden plot, courtesy of the Miller Brothers Farm in Southport near Miller Street. Looking east, Maple Avenue is behind the students.

McLeod Building. The 37th face from the right is C. Albert Janowski, grandfather of author Diane L. Janowski.

During the trouble on the Mexican border, Mrs. Harriet Tuttle Arnot Rathbone was one of the pioneers in developing the Canteen Service of Elmira. Mrs. Rathbone personally saw to it that men who passed through Elmira to the south received a kindly greeting and refreshments. The service was organized on May 29, 1918, and the first troop train was served strawberry ice cream on Saturday, June 1. Trains were served from 5 a.m. until 11:30 p.m. Every man received a fully equipped comfort kit from the canteen. Comfort kits contained a variety of the following: sandwiches, candy bars, crackers, tobacco, cigarettes, magazines, newspapers, oranges, apples, and pears. Over 200,000 servicemen were served milk, coffee, soda pop, doughnuts, soup, eggs, ice cream, and cookies. This photo, c. 1918, was taken on the steps of the George Personius Photography Studio at 269 Baldwin Street.

The Elmira-Chemung County Welcoming Committee awaited the World War I homecoming of Company L on Lackawanna Train #4 on April 1, 1919.

Soldiers pose with coffins in front of the armory on East Church Street. One hundred and four Elmirans were killed in the Great War. The first Elmiran killed was Pvt. Francis Higby, a 1911 graduate of Elmira Free Academy. He left behind a young widow and his mother, Mrs. Bertha Page, who lived at 138 West Water Street.

The Homecoming Parade for Company L was held on April 1, 1919. On homecoming day, schools and factories were closed early, and thousands of Elmirans met the train at the depot. Bells and whistles sounded at 3 p.m. As Lackawanna Train #4 arrived at 4:30 p.m. the big siren on city hall wailed. The procession paused briefly at the armory, then marched under the Victory Arch over North Main Street.

A conscientious Willys-Morrow employee inspects Prestwich Fluid Gauges.

This is the corner of Main and Water Streets looking south. The bridge was closed to automobiles in 1920, but remained open to pedestrian traffic. On the right is the Kelly Drugstore at 201 West Water Street that was run by brothers John P., Charles F., and E. Leslie Kelly. The new bridge opened on December 21, 1921, and survived until 1974. The buildings on either side in this photo were razed for access to subsequent bridge constructions.

The south end of the Main Street Bridge is seen before its demolition in 1920 in this photo by Fred Loomis.

In team sports like baseball, the public found games which reflected "the working together for a common goal" attitude of the Industrial Age. Amateur teams consisting of neighbors, friends, and co-workers provided an outlet for competitive feelings and a means for gathering socially outside the job. The Eclipse Machine Company's team were the Southern Tier champions in 1919, winning ten games and losing only two. (Quotation from *Mark Twain's Elmira* by Michelle L. Cotton.)

Elmira College students strike a pose during the annual May Day celebration, c. 1926.

Cartoning, casing, and wrapping at the F.M. Howell Co. are seen in this July 20, 1919 picture. Founded in 1883 by Fred M. Howell and always located at the south end of the Lake Street Bridge, the F.M. Howell Co. first printed and manufactured cigar boxes. As the regional tobacco industry receded, Howell added menus, labels, and folding boxes to the company's product list. One of Elmira's most vital and oldest companies, the Howell Co. has kept pace with the packaging industry to include pharmaceuticals, advertising design, and specialty packaging.

The Perfect Laundry was owned by John Danaher and William Manning and was located at 115 West Church Street.

Art Naglee sits at the wheel of his father's 1914 Selden moving van, one of the first trucks in the area. Sam Naglee founded his moving company in 1912. Naglee Moving & Storage is still located in Chemung County. Art Naglee stops by frequently to talk about the old days.

Seen here are employees of the Willys-Morrow Company on South Main Street. From 1907 until 1934, the Morrow Manufacturing Company, and later the Willys-Morrow Co., produced drill chucks, machine parts and tools, transmissions, universal joints, gears, ball bearings, nuts, and bolts for Overland and Willys-Knight cars. Peak production was during World War I when 6,500 people worked in the Elmira plant.

The Star Department Store was located at South Main Street and Pennsylvania Avenue on Elmira's southside. The store was owned by Christian R. Mosch. By 1923, Mosch had closed this location and reopened as C.R. Mosch Clothiers at 114 Lake Street. The building in this photo also served as a theatre from 1914 to 1917. The man on the left is Lynn Dickinson, a Star clerk who became a well-known real estate agent by 1925. The woman third from the right is Dorothy Baldwin, a Star clerk who lived at 208 W. Henry Street. Currently, this is the site of the Byrne Dairy Store, just north of Bernie Murray's Restaurant.

This was William H. Webb's Marketeria Store located at 115 North Main Street in 1924. In the photo are, from left to right, William H. Webb, LaMont Webb, and George Cleveland, who lived with the Webb family at 914 West First Street. The caption on the photo reads "First Big Store." The store's slogan was "Serve Yourself Original" (see p. 94). The Marketeria was located in the Synder Building, which has been occupied by a variety of retailers. Now known as the Midtown Building, it serves as the headquarters for the Panosian family's many businesses.

Hank Sheely's Corn Eating Contest. Aug. 12. 1921.

On Friday afternoon, August 12, 1921, at Hank (Henry B.) and Mamie Sheely's home at 1050 Pennsylvania Avenue, Masonic friends were pleasantly entertained at an annual get-together. Guests enjoyed a sumptuous "corn and wiener dinner." Dominoes, quoits, baseball, and cribbage were played. Among the distinguished guests was Frank E. Tripp, founder of Gannett newspapers, sitting at the head of the table on the right. Hank Sheely was a farmer and the proprietor of the Broadway Driving range. His farm, located from Cedar Street to Bulkhead, was sold in 1925, and the area became Carter, Sheely, Haskell, and Sliter Streets. His home at the corner of Pennsylvania and Spruce Street became the Olthof Funeral Home. The photo is looking at the southside of the house with Pennsylvania Avenue on the right (see p. 70).

St. Luke's Vacation Bible School is shown here at the corner of Lake and Division Streets. This church is still in use as the New Hope Missionary Church.

The Hedding Methodist Episcopal Church was dedicated in 1852 and named for Elijah Hedding. This photo is the Hedding M.E. Church Men's Class on February 17, 1924.

Elmira College students pose for a tableau.

The Misses Norton, Emily, Frances, and Mary conducted a private kindergarten in a small house at the northeast corner of College and Second Streets. The school ran for 42 years until it closed in 1928. Over the years, it enrolled 587 students. This c. 1922 photo was taken at the pond at Elmira College.

Public parks were the pride of Elmira. Hoffman's Grove was purchased by the city in 1886 from George McCann for $15,000. Known to generations of Elmirans as Grove Park, it continues this kind of activity through the Summer Cohesion program.

The Neighborhood House at 669 Dickinson Street had programs and activities for the children of Elmira's eastside. Vocational guidance, homemaking skills, art, music, and sports were among its offerings. On the far left in this c. 1925 photo is Ray Hulbert, who was active at the Neighborhood House from 1919 to World War II. In 1977, the Neighborhood House moved nearby to a modern facility on Fifth Street (see p. 62).

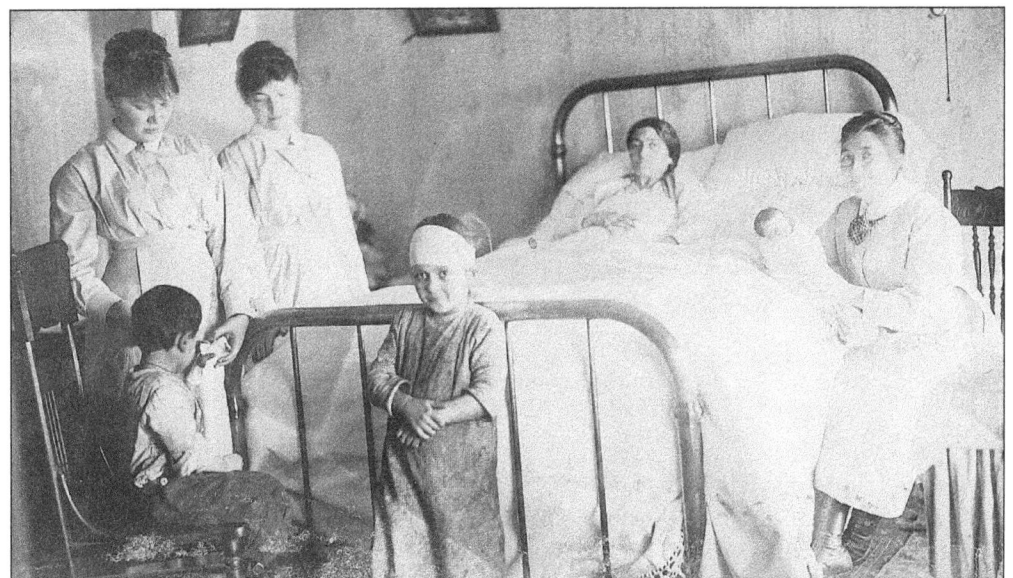

Bedside comfort was part of the Visiting Nurses program, as can be seen in this pre-1925 photo.

The Orphan's Home on Franklin Street was begun in 1868 through the efforts of the Ladies Relief Association. The home operated without state aid; only charitable gifts and the receipts of an annual festival kept it alive. Music was an important feature at the home, which offered pianos, victrolas, and music lessons. Girls learned housework and sewing. Boys sawed wood and brought in coal. In 1880, two groups of Elmira orphans, totaling about 30, were sent to Red Cloud, Nebraska, for adoption, traveling via the famous "orphan trains." This area is now an open yard near St. Mary's Church. (Photo by Fred T. Loomis.)

In the days before school buses, some students went to school on trolleys. In this 1927 photo, high school students get off the trolley at the corner of East Clinton Street and Lake Street to go to classes at Elmira Free Academy (now Ernie Davis Junior High School). In the background is the Borst & Cuffney Drug Store at 531 Lake Street and the Samuel Haddad Grocery at 529 Lake Street.

Budding actors at the Hendy Avenue School in 1928 perform the operetta *The Pantry Cook and the Pirate.*

Built in 1873, the old Chemung County Jail was a brick-and-stone structure that was showing its age by the 1930s. In 1938, the state ordered that it must be replaced. The present jail opened in 1941.

The Harry B. Bentley Post 443, American Legion of Elmira, Drum and Bugle Corps was organized in 1929. Post 443 sponsored an annual midnight parade on the eve of Armistice Day and ended the festivities with a bonfire at Wisner Park. The Eternal Light at the Veterans Memorial in Wisner Park was given to Elmira by Post 443.

In 1927, William H. Webb owned and operated three grocery stores. This store was located at 57 South Main Street, at the corner of Chemung Place. Webb's son LaMont stands in front. The other two stores were located at 209 West Water Street and 569 East Water Street. The Webb family had previously owned the Marketeria Store at 115 North Main Street (see p. 86). The storefront pictured is now the Renaissance Beauty Salon at 57 1/2 South Main Street.

These Girl Scouts spent time at Camp Iroquois in August 1929. The tall girl on the left is Joan Lewis French. The Girl Scout movement started in Elmira in 1917, and, by 1927, there were 450 scouts.

The Federation Building was initiated by a group of prominent Elmira women in 1905. The building cost $60,000 and opened in 1908. This cafeteria, c. 1930, was on the second floor. This is the present location of Steele Memorial Library.

Employees of the new Mark Twain Hotel are pictured here shortly after its opening on March 23, 1929. All the individuals are unknown except the young man at the top left, Stanley Rybak. Stanley worked for the hotel until 1969 as head waiter. After retirement, he was employed at Rybak's Grill on Washington Avenue at Hatch Street. Stanley's wife, Rose, also worked at the Mark Twain Hotel until at least 1973. Stanley still lives in Elmira.

Prior to the elevation of the Erie Railroad tracks in 1934, photographers accurately surveyed the area affected. These are remarkably clear photos with exquisite visual detail of Elmira during the Depression years.

This is Sullivan Street looking north from the grade level crossing, just below East Avenue, c. 1930. In the distance, on the left, is the Roy R. Welch Grocery at 651 Sullivan Street. Several of the houses on the right still stand in the shadow of the elevated railroad.

The largest celebration in local history to date was held on August 29, 1929, and was the 150th anniversary of the Battle of Newtown. There was a huge pageant and mock battle at the base of East Hill (the site of a golf course). Overhead, the Navy dirigible *Los Angeles* was watched by a crowd estimated at 75,000. In the parking lot, every car looked the same.

This picture shows Newtown Creek Bridge at East Water Street looking west. The Arnot Mill is at the right, with the Delaware, Lackawanna, & Western Railroad tracks just beyond the bridge. In 1930, the railroad and creek were bridged, doing away with the grade level crossing. (Photo by Fred T. Loomis.)

This view of North Main Street, looking north from Water Street, shows downtown Elmira in the midst of the Depression. In the late 1930s, one of the many Works Progress Administration projects was the removal of the trolley tracks.

The Mark Twain Food Market was opened by four Elmirans in 1933 and lasted for 26 years at 154 North Main Street.

A jovial Rotarian group celebrates the "Glad" County by wearing rubber boots and holding farm tools. This photo was taken c. 1938. Ransom Lewis (far right), the president of Elmira Precision Tool, lived at 412 W. Clinton Street. Also in this group are Clair Schneck, who sold washing machines and refrigerators at 203 Lake and lived at 809 W. Church Street, and Clarence Stewart, manager of the New Method Varnish Company at 609 W. Water Street.

American LaFrance began when Truckson LaFrance joined forces with the Elmira Union Iron Works and regional financiers and in 1873 built a small plant to manufacture fire engines. At the company's peak, it employed 1,000 Elmirans at its factory on Elmira's southside. Imagine the sound in this room.

American Airways was the first air carrier in our region. Their flights began here in 1933 and were discontinued in 1937. Shown here are passengers boarding an American Airways Curtiss airplane on the grass at the airport in Big Flats.

The American Airways Landing Field began operations on June 24, 1933. Later, it became the Elmira Airport, then the Chemung County Airport, and it is now the Elmira-Corning Regional Airport.

Harris Hill is known as the "Glider Capital of the World." In 1930–31, the first National Gliding and Soaring Championships were held there. The peculiar lay of the land and the nature of the air currents make it ideal for this sport.

The Chemung County Airport had its origins in 1933 as a grassy field used for landing emergencies. In 1940, it was designated as a Defense Landing Area by the federal government. In 1941, the board of directors authorized $590,000 for the construction of the airport here. Three hardsurfaced runways with lighting were installed by the federal government. Some airlines associated with the airport's history are American, United, Empire, Mohawk, US Airways, and Northwest.

On October 25, 1933, the first Erie train moved over the temporary train bridge during the project to elevate the tracks through the city. This view is at the corner of Water Street and Railroad Avenue. Prior to 1933 the railroad was at street level. This construction disrupted the lives of all Elmirans and rail travelers. The railroad elevation project opened eastbound on June 25, 1934, and westbound on October 2, 1934. The building on the left is Frieman's Curtain Shop.

This is a view looking north on Railroad Avenue at Water Street, c. 1932, before the elevation of the tracks. Some businesses of interest on the left are A. Schulte Cigars at 100 West Water Street and on Railroad Avenue; Cooper Wall Paper at 111–113; the Army and Navy Surplus at 123; and the Inter Hotel Storage (in the Richardson Shoe Building) at 125. On the right are F&W Grand Silver at 100 East Water and the James Reynolds Tobacco Warehouse beyond. The railroad was elevated in 1934. Presently, on the left is Harold's and on the right is WETM-TV.

This photo was made during the elevation of the Erie Railroad tracks in 1933–34. Trolley car patrons had to clamber over the construction from West Water Street to East Water Street to continue on the route. This view is looking west from the roof of the Kobacker Store (where WETM-TV is now located). (Photo courtesy of the *Star Gazette*.)

A short traffic tie-up occurred while the Gray Street crossing was briefly closed for railroad elevation work in 1934. On the right is Kelly's Service Station at 105 West Gray Street (where the Centertown Parking Garage entrance is now). George Gunn was the manager. By the 1930s, traffic and parking had become serious problems for the downtown business district. The popularity of individual transportation combined with an extremely successful retail environment led to urban development in the 1950s.

Mary Welles Mooers Smith (mother of author Allen C. Smith), of the Womens' Ambulance and Defense Corps (WADC), serves breakfast to an unknown serviceman at the WADC lounge at the Erie Railroad Station, c. 1943.

During World War II, the mayor's committee maintained canteens in both the Lackawanna and Erie Railroad stations. These women were members of the Volunteer Corps led by Catherine Finter (at right). Ms. Finter was a physical fitness instructor at Elmira College and lived at 311 Irvine Place.

Miss Mae Leavitt passes out morale boosting posters for distribution in Chemung County. Miss Leavitt was a director of the Grey Ladies during World War II. She lived at 810 Euclid Avenue.

The U.S. Army, in 1941, purchased 550 acres north of Horseheads for use as a supply base to be called the Horseheads Holding and Reconsignment Point. Within a few months, construction for a storage facility began. Vast amounts of World War II material (tanks, cars, war equipment) were stored here for the June 1944 invasion of Europe. After the war, the Horseheads building boom continued. The new Victory Heights apartment complex housed many families. Horseheads began developing in every direction. Industries sprang up, including Westinghouse Electric Tube Inc., bringing many new people to the area and creating the need for Windsor Gardens. (Photo courtesy of the War Department.)

Brothers John and Blaine Hazlett operated the Frank R. Hazlett Grocery Store until 1957. It was located at 224 Oakwood Avenue in Elmira Heights. This building now houses the Heights Laundry.

Michael J. Diveris makes a special sundae at The Aster in 1943.

Three
YEARS OF PROSPERITY

In this c. 1935 photo, trolley fare was 7¢. Elmira's trolleys were replaced with buses in 1939. Rush hours were between 7–8 a.m. and 4–5 p.m., when the trolleys were packed. (Photo courtesy of the *Star Gazette*.)

Elmira's Victory metal scrap drive collected fences, tin cans, pots, and pans. The collection bins were located in Wisner Park, and Langdon Plaza is in the background.

Pepsi-Cola displays its fine product at a Food Show in Elmira in 1939.

Thomas P. and Gus Greven were the founders of The Aster in 1916. This famous candy kitchen was a landmark of the East Water and Lake Streets area (it was first located at 335 East Water Street). Later, John K. Diveris and Peter J. Pappas purchased it (then located at 329 East Water), and Thomas Greven established The Nut Shop candy store a few doors away. John Diveris continued making candy into the late 1950s. He and Mrs. Diveris made ribbon candy, hard candy, cream candy, and chocolate-covered molasses chips. One of their employees was their son Kosmos, who later was involved in education and politics. From left to right are Marjorie Dana, Louis Padokis, Peter Pappas, Nancy ?, and James Pappas. The business closed in 1966.

John K. Diveris stands in front of The Aster at 329 East Water Street. The *Sun Triangle* sculpture on Water Street marks the approximate former location of The Aster.

Employees work the line at American LaFrance (ALF). During its tenure in Elmira, American LaFrance was credited with production of 60 percent of the fire apparatus in service in the United States and Canada. During World War II, ALF built Air Force crash trucks, aircraft oxygen cylinders, fire extinguishers for military hardware, landing gear parts, and gun mounts.

An unidentified woman operates a drill press at Remington Rand during World War II.

On May 28, 1946, women wade across Water Street at Main. After nearly 5 inches of rain in 5 days, the Chemung River rose 23 feet above normal and overflowed its banks once again. All of downtown was underwater. At Lake and Carroll Streets, water measured 30 inches deep. Thirty-two homes were destroyed, and a child drowned near Dunn Field. Three hundred families needed assistance in the form of food, clothing, shelter, and home repair.

The spring of 1946 brought weather disasters to Elmira. In May, the Chemung River flooded. The first week of June brought a tornado that raged through the city. Three days later, a windstorm felled hundreds of weakened trees. At Elmira Free Academy, a large tree crashed against the building, breaking windows, scattering glass, and instantly killing the class valedictorian, Barbara Jane Crawford, a beautiful and well-liked student.

This is the pattern-making room at American Bridge, a division of the U.S. Steel Corporation, c. 1955. Notable projects from this plant included the steel for the Tappan Zee and Verrazano Bridges, the Apollo Launch Complex at the Kennedy Space Center, Disney World, and the Belmont Race Track. Currently, the facility is occupied by AdTranz Corp.

Employees of Remington Rand assemble typewriters in the former Morrow Plant building on South Main Street. Remington Rand manufactured office machines in Elmira from 1935 until 1971 and had 4,000 employees during its peak.

John Brand was a major tobacco grower living on Elmira's southside. From his personal property, he gave the land for Riverside Park, which was renamed by the city in his honor. The first Brand Park Swimming Pool opened in the early 1900s but was destroyed in the flood of 1946. It was rebuilt in 1948, and still entertains Elmirans during hot summers.

Robert Long spent his childhood summers from 1909 to 1916 helping his father operate the first Long carousel at the park. The Long family were pioneers in the American carousel industry. Into their late 70s, Mr. and Mrs. Long operated the carousel, other rides, and much of the park's daily activities.

Elmira did its part in the wartime effort. We were ranked 12th in the nation for our production of wartime equipment. Pictured here are employees at the Eclipse Machine Division of Bendix Corporation in Elmira Heights. The company's peak year was 1943, when three shifts employed 8,594 men and women. Known as the "Arsenal of Democracy," Eclipse originally manufactured bicycle brakes and engine starters. During the war, Eclipse converted to ordnance and made fuel injection pumps for B-29s, automatic time fuses for anti-aircraft shells, 20mm aircraft cannon, and magnetos for aircraft.

Here, the strength of products made in Elmira are proven for the safety of firemen everywhere. American LaFrance made the first "spring rising aerial ladder truck." In 1941, ALF built the first 125-foot aerial ladder for Boston, Massachusetts. The mobile aerial platform was developed in the 1960s.

The Benedictine Monks celebrate the Mass of Dedication at Mount Saviour in 1953.

After their shifts ended, the Riverside Power Plant Employees' Band got together to make music. In this 1952 photo are, from left to right, foreman Henry Budnick (residence at 517 Morley Place), Fred Krapp (residence at 701 Pattinson), Pete Carozza, Ralph Birger, Ray Updike (residence at 2 Symonds Place), Ralph Gray (residence at 24 Sunnyside Drive), Walt Gublo (residence at 1010 College Avenue), and safety director Roy Stauffer (residence at 116 Lexington Avenue).

Holiday decorating for downtown Elmira was a community project in 1954. This view looks up North Main Street from West Water Street. The perfect gifts were easy to find in Elmira's 749 retail stores and businesses.

Winter weather hinders Christmas shopping in 1954 on Main Street at Market, looking north. The dark building on the right is the Mark Twain Hotel. On the extreme right is S.F. Iszard's, founded in 1922. Iszard's was famous for its Christmas parade, which drew thousands downtown annually.

The Lake Street Bridge was temporarily closed in 1959 and replaced with a modern span in 1961. Now the oldest of the five city bridges, it is still in use today. Standing in the center is Mayor Edward A. Mooers (grandfather of author Allen C. Smith).

Elmira was on the main Erie Railroad passenger train route from New York City to Chicago. Passenger trains drew less and less patronage owing to automobile and airline travel in the 1960s, and, in January 1970, the last Erie-Lackawanna train left our depot.

Scouts hike to Rorick's Glen, c. 1960. In 1944, the Boy Scouts acquired Rorick's Glen and rehabilitated the site for use by the scouts. It was a beautiful site for scout activities.

This is an aerial view of the Chemung County Fairgrounds on June 5, 1976. The activity in the infield is the very popular Scoutorama, sponsored by the Sullivan Trail Council Boy Scouts of America.

Ernest Randolph Davis (#44) was born on December 14, 1939, in Uniontown, Pennsylvania. Ernie's father was killed before he was born, and he lived with his grandmother until age 11, when he came to Elmira to live with his mother, Mrs. Marie Davis Radford Fleming. Ernie liked all organized sports programs for children. At Elmira Free Academy, he played basketball, football, and baseball. He was well liked at school, and was voted sophomore class president, junior prom king, and student council president. One of the reasons he chose to attend Syracuse University in 1958 was so that his mother could go to his games. Ernie won the coveted Heisman Trophy in 1961 and had signed a contract with the Cleveland Browns but was diagnosed with leukemia in July 1962. He died on May 18, 1963, before he played one professional game. Elmira has honored his memory with Ernie Davis Junior High School, Ernie Davis Park, and a life-sized bronze sculpture near the site of his boyhood home.

In 1961, Paul Prunier, a teacher at Broadway School, taught local history to bright and eager students from the newly published Chemung County history book.

This picture looks north on State Street toward the Elmira Theatre with its beautifullylighted marquis. The street was eventually widened on both sides to make way for the Clemens Center Parkway.

The Centertown Park & Shop area opened in 1959 with 540 parking spaces. Market Street and Railroad Avenue were closed, and, by 1962, 17 old buildings had been razed for this parking lot. Newberry's, which opened in the mid-1920s, expanded in 1953 and again in 1963. All but two of the business buildings (Harold's and Rosenbaum's) shown in this *c.* 1960 photo were demolished by 1998.

On the morning of June 23, 1972, flood volunteers push a car in front of old Southside High School at the intersection of Pennsylvania Avenue and South Main Street. The building on the left originally served as Independent Hose Company #3 (see p. 72, top).

Immediately after the waters receded, looting began. National Guardsmen prevented travel over the Main Street Bridge and protected the business district. Residents were not allowed to return to survey their ruined homes for several days due to threats of gas leaks, fires, electrocution, and other hazards. Since 1972, the Main Street Bridge has been replaced and the building has been razed for Riverfront Park.

The 1972 flood's fury at Franklin Street and South Avenue can be seen here. The river rose a foot higher than the dike. Elmira's southside became a primary channel for the powerful flow of the Chemung. Cars tumbled in the wild current. Old Southside High School can be seen in the background. (Photo courtesy of the *Elmira Star Gazette*.)

The flood was at its peak when this aerial photo was taken at midday on June 23, 1972. The view is looking southeast at the bend in the river. Many of the houses in the foreground were deemed unsafe for human use and were torn down during urban renewal.

Southsiders driven from their homes carry belongings to Southside High School. Rising water eventually forced them to reevacuate. On the far left of this photo are Robert Janowski and Anna Roemelt, father and great aunt of author Diane L. Janowski. (Photo courtesy of the *Elmira Star Gazette*.)

During the flood of 1972, the old steel bridge at Walnut Street was broken apart and washed away. On September 30, 1974, the new Walnut Street Bridge opened.

The large building was built by George Curtis in 1917 and occupied for many years variously by Curtis, Flickinger, Brady Electric, and Banfield-Jennings-Baker. Elmirans remember it as Banfield-Baker in the 1960s and 1970s, when they had a monkey and a talking bird. Everything in this photo except for the Aluminum Doors sign had been demolished by 1998. It is now the area of the new post office and bus station.

South Main Street shops just below Henry Street are pictured here in March 1975. The structures were razed to make way for the Southport Towers apartment complex. The Southside Sub Shop is still in business on South Main.

This is East Water Street in 1973. Elmira wanted a new look. In an effort to incorporate the Chemung River with downtown, all of the buildings on the south side of Water Street, east of Main, were demolished. Riverfront Park, landscaped with walkways, benches, artificial streams, and fountains, replaced these turn-of-the-century structures.

This view looks north at the intersection of Park Place, North Main, and Third Street in 1972 (see p. 26).

Employees at the Ann Page Plant, located in the town of Horseheads, process and inspect candy for delivery to A&P stores in the east. Development and construction of the 1.5-million-square-foot plant was begun in secrecy in 1964. During the company's peak years, 2,300 persons from the community were employed preparing mayonnaise, salad dressing, peanut butter, Spanish olives, macaroni, jam, desserts, candy, soup, and beans. Economic reversals of the 1970s caused the project to close.

Urban renewal of the 1970s removed more than 700 old houses, primarily on Elmira's eastside, and replaced them with new low-income housing developments.

The carousel at Eldridge Park is a fond memory in the hearts of many Elmirans. The brass ring meant another exciting and romantic ride.

The Speedway Roller Coaster at Eldridge Park is seen here during the attraction's heyday in the 1950s and 1960s.

In 1978, a Clemens Center employee washes the city grime from the mirrored facade. Our remaining grand old buildings are few and far between, and juxtaposed with unique new buildings and acres of vacant city land, they create an unusual downtown landscape.